ABOVE: *A Britains special casting and painting order of the 1930s for a contemporary collector: the Fife and Drum Band of the Royal Welch Fusiliers.*

COVER: *Part of a coronation procession: a converted band of the Royal Horse Artillery precedes Britains New Metal Scots Guards. The buildings are by Tri-ang Spot-on (Cotswold Village series), and the roadway by Dinky Way.*

TOY SOLDIERS

James Opie

Shire Publications Ltd

CONTENTS

Printed in Great Britain by C. I. Thomas & Sons (Haverfordwest) Ltd, Press Buildings, Merlins Bridge, Haverfordwest, Dyfed SA61 1XF.

Note: In the captions to all the photographs the soldiers are described from left to right.

ACKNOWLEDGEMENTS

Many collectors have directly or indirectly contributed to the subject matter of this book. Where there are matters in doubt or differences of opinion the views expressed are the author's own. The author is grateful to all those who have helped his researches and pays tribute to their friendliness. The lower photograph on page 6 is reproduced by kind permission of Britains Ltd.

ABOVE: *Magnificent 60 millimetre Marx Romans in plastic.*

BELOW: *A converted Royal Marine band, based on Britains figures, including plastic Eyes Right, for example the front row of drummers.*

Brigader solid toy soldiers, 48 millimetre scale: Danish-made models of the Livgarde of Denmark. In real life these soldiers are cadets, and the models capture this well. The tin sentry boxes are distinctive of the Tivoli Palace in Copenhagen.

INTRODUCTION

Toy soldiers have been produced in their millions by every industrial nation. They provide a social record, reflecting their age and origin. Being manufactured and collected en masse, they give a feeling of great armies which the more individualistic 'military model' lacks. They are evocative of pleasant days of childhood, spent on the floor playing uncomplicated wargames. Furthermore, although not many of them are strictly accurate models, they are often wonderfully quaint and a joy to the eye.

Toy soldiers are defined as miniature military figures commercially produced and distributed as children's playthings. Many other objects of similar appearance but with different purposes have been made through the ages. These include Egyptian tomb furniture, to provide Pharaohs with suitable armies in the afterlife, and some of this may be seen in

the British Museum. Miniature chariots, soldiers and figures were often handmade from wood, clay or soft metal throughout the classical period. In medieval times, when noblemen were trained from birth as warriors, models were created to teach the finer points of jousting. Later, for early lessons in generalship, prospective kings of France manoeuvred beautifully made armies of pure silver, all later melted down to swell the coffers of the French Revolution.

Thus the making of miniature soldiers has a long history and when industrial societies grew up mass production began and the first true toy soldiers were made. First to appear were the flat tin soldiers; then came solid fully round figures, followed by the hollow-cast models, with many other processes being tried with varying degrees of success.

ABOVE: *Scale in toy soldiers is measured by the height of an infantryman in millimetres to the top of the head without the hat. Demonstrated here by Britains figures are various scales: (from left to right) HH size, 83 millimetres; H size, 70 millimetres; standard size, 54 millimetres; early Britains, 52 millimetres; W size, 45 millimetres; B size, 44 millimetres; and two very small cavalry, 35 millimetres. Standard size is the equivalent of a gauge 1 model railway and is 1/32 life size. Model railway 00 gauge is 1/72 life size and equivalent to a toy soldier scale of 20 millimetres.*

BELOW: *Flat toy soldiers. These are 28 millimetre scale Ochel flats engraved by Frank in the 1930s. They represent the Royal Scots Greys at the battle of Waterloo and were presented free in packets of Greys cigarettes in place of cigarette cards. The thickness of flats can be seen in the third figure from the left, which is viewed end on. The delicate engraving can clearly be seen on these unpainted castings.*

BOTTOM: *Heyde solid toy soldiers. A group of military railway engineers in 48 millimetre scale. Heyde was famous for groups of action figures.*

4

A selection of solid toy soldiers. (Back row) All Mignot except the soldier on the camel, which is German-made. Note the Mignot standard bearer's head, which, as with many solid figures, is plugged in at the neck. (Front row) Italian Papal Guard; German-made portrait figure, possibly of Kitchener; a 20 millimetre scale Heyde lancer; Eriksson models of seventeenth-century musketeer and pikeman; another lancer; and a Heyde British Camel Corps trooper.

METHODS OF MANUFACTURE

Seven methods have been widely used in manufacturing toy soldiers throughout the world. These are:

1. *Flat casting in tin alloy.* This is the earliest form of the commercial mass-produced toy soldier. It began around 1730, but flats are still being made today. They have always been a German speciality. Once manufacturers became experienced, the detail engraved on the surface of the models was, and is, astonishing. The figures are wafer thin, under a millimetre thick, and from an end-on view can hardly be seen.

The variety of these figures is enormous. Some are cast with extra legs and arms, so that those not needed can be broken off and thus a variety of different poses can be obtained from one mould. Some of the sets issued comprised hundreds of figures, such as Alexander and the Persians with 220 pieces. Three of the

leading manufacturers, all German, with the approximate dates between which production took place, are: Allgeyer (1790-1896), Heinrichsen (1830-1945), Ochel (1925 to the present).

2. *Solid casting in lead alloy.* This is the process favoured by European manufacturers for fully modelled figures. The models are much heavier than those produced by any other process. First commercially made in France about 1790, these figures are fully three-dimensional. Modern technology with rubber moulds has brought the solid figure back into favour, and many manufacturers throughout the world have used this method.

Prominent manufacturers include: Lucotte (France, 1790-1900), Mignot (France, 1830 to the present), Heyde (Germany, 1870-1944), Heinrich (Germany, 1870-1920), Brigader (Denmark,

ABOVE: *A hollow-casting mould. This is a Johillco mould which fits together to form a toy dog. It is upside down, as the pouring hole can be seen at the bottom of each side. The mould is in four pieces that close together with the flick of a wrist. After the mould has been turned over to pour out again, and then reopened, the toy is left on the central piece of the mould that forms the belly of the dog. In the foreground is a plaster mould of a Johillco pirate, part of the process of transferring the master figure into a brass mould such as the one behind. An example of the finished toy pirate has been fitted into the mould to show its shape better.*

BELOW: *Britains' casting shop. The men take molten alloy out of their tanks and pour swiftly into their moulds, and the piles of castings grow rapidly. Boys top up the tanks on the call of the casters, each of whom gives a recognisable individual signal to 'fill up'.*

Semi-flat toy soldiers. On the left are three 48 millimetre scale home-cast cavalrymen, the third one turned round to show the thickness. Behind the cavalry are typical home-cast German bandsmen. To the right are a modern brochure advertising home casting kits from the Prins August company, and contemporary groups of figures depicting the Boer War and the Sino-Japanese War. Semi-flat casting lends itself to the casting of large pieces of scenery like the blazing Chinese pavilion shown, and Britains produced most of their metal trees in this way.

1946 to the present), Authenticast (Ireland, 1947-50), Figir (Italy, 1927 to the present), MIM (Belgium, 1935-48), Alymer (Spain, 1928 to the present).

3. *Hollow casting in lead alloy.* This process was invented by the Britain family and was the dominant form of manufacture in Britain and the United States from 1893 to the late 1950s. Hollow casting is done by pouring an alloy of lead, tin and antimony into a slightly cooler mould, so that a skin forms round the outside of the shape. The antimony expands on cooling to give a crisp casting without the support of solid metal, and the still liquid metal in the centre of the mould is quickly poured out again, leaving a hollow figure. A skilled operator might produce three hundred figures an hour from a hand-held mould. Hollow-cast models are light for their size and have little holes in their heads, feet or other suitable places, through which the molten metal was poured out again.

Leading manufacturers were, in Britain: Britains (1893-1966), Reka (1900-33), Hanks (1900-14), BMC (1918-25), Renvoize (1900-14), Fry (1905-25), Johillco (1900-57), Timpo (1949-56), Crescent (1930-57), Cherilea (1949-59), and in the United States, the so called 'dime store' manufacturers Barclay (1924-65) and Manoil (1930-55).

4. *Semi-flat casting, in pure lead or alloy.* This method is intermediate between flat casting and solid casting and has been used by a variety of manufacturers alongside other methods. Some companies have produced moulds for casting this type of toy soldier at home, and these are the examples most normally seen. Lacking the detail of solid or hollow casting, or the delicate engraving of flat casting, semi-flat figures are cheap and easy to produce, and usually worthless, since few collectors enjoy them. They feel heavy and usually look ugly, with heads too small in proportion. End-on, they are about 3-4 millimetres (⅛ inch) thick.

Manufacturers issuing home casting moulds include the Ideal Mould Company (United Kingdom, 1930-40) and Prince August (Sweden, 1958 to the present).

5. *Compression moulding in composition on wire.* This process originated in Germany, and the figures look as if they are made of plaster. 'Composition' is a mixture of sawdust, casein, kaolin, dextrin and bone glue, pressed wet into a mould around a wire skeleton, which often goes rusty if exposed by cracks or breakage. Usually these toys are larger scale (70 millimetres, 2¾ inches) than those made by other methods.

Composition manufacturers include:

7

ABOVE: *Composition toy soldiers. (Back row) Various Italian-made types, Papal ceremonial dress, a redshirt and Garibaldi, and on the extreme right a Chinese horseman, made in China. (Centre row) Three of the famous 1930s Elastolin German army figures; two Elastolin Swiss army bandsmen, from the time when German army models were forbidden, during the allied occupation; three splendid Elastolin models of the British army in full dress; small and large scale Lineol Wehrmacht figures; and an Elastolin model of a Norwegian standard bearer. (Front row). An unidentified figure; a Durso Belgian horse grenadier standard bearer; a group of five British-made TAG figures; and two rather crude British infantry by an unknown British manufacturer, the ends of the guns being formed of ordinary pins; and on the extreme right a Leyla figure. The majority of the composition figures are in 70 millimetre scale, the usual size for this process.*

BELOW: *A box of archetypal toy soldiers by Wend-Al. The uniforms are fictional. These are some of the moulds that Wend-Al borrowed from Quiralu.*

Elastolin (Germany, 1904-55), Lineol (Germany, 1935-45), Durso (Belgium, 1935-50), Figur Brevett (Italy, 1956-66).

6. *Sand casting in aluminium.* This method was pioneered by Quiralu in France and also used by Wend-Al in Britain during the 1950s. Toy soldiers produced by sand casting are more nearly indestructible than those produced by any other method. The models tend to be thicker than other types, feel light and give a distinctive clink when knocked together. Quiralu and Wend-Al are the two major manufacturers.

7. *Injection moulding in plastic.* This has been the dominant form of production throughout the world since the late 1950s, because plastic is much cheaper than metal and the moulding technique can be automated. Contrary to popular belief, plastic soldiers are not indestructible; they range from tough to fragile, and many do not last as long as metal ones. Many different types of plastic are used, and flat, semi-flat and fully round models are all possible.

Major manufacturers include: Britains (Herald) (UK, 1953 to the present), Timpo (UK, 1956-79), Lone Star (UK, 1954-73), Crescent (UK, 1956-80), Cherilea (UK, 1956-78), Airfix (UK, 1964 to the present), Marx (USA, 1953-79), Starlux (France, 1947 to the present), Elastolin (Germany; 1947-84), Reamsa (Spain, 1955-78), Atlantic (Italy, 1972 to the present).

Apart from the above, toy soldiers have been made by every conceivable method. Paper cutouts, die casting, wood carving, card, pressed tin and foam rubber are just a few of the processes and materials. The seven methods already described, however, probably account for 95 per cent of all the toy soldiers ever produced.

Worldwide toy soldiers in all sorts of materials. (Top row) Three Russian-made Red Army bandsmen made of china; an American Barclay 'pod foot' marine; two other Barclay figures; a zinc alloy die-cast figure; an Italian-made foam-rubber Alpini ski trooper; an Italian-made aluminium ski trooper; and a very ancient looking solid French soldier on a wire loop base, which could be a hundred years old. (Middle row) A Ping figure of Oliver Cromwell; a cardboard rifleman; a Japanese idea of a Scottish figure and a samurai by Minikin of Japan; the group to the right are British-made tinplate figures, lithographed and stamped out. (Bottom row) A large wooden French Imperial Guard; a Belgian-made MIM figure of a Roman bowman; a French-made hollow-cast portrayal of Napoleon (a favourite subject); a Chad Valley paper on plywood 17th Lancer, followed by two other paper on wood groups. Second from the right is a pressed tinplate infantryman with the two halves held together with tin tabs. Extreme right is a large hollow-cast German-made model of a British grenadier. For size comparison, the Japanese soldier third in the middle row is the standard 54 millimetre size.

ABOVE: *'Germanic' figures. The Britains figures in this photograph are all in the middle row. The rest of the figures, including the second from the left in the middle row, are either German-made hollowcasts or copies of Britains models by other British makers. The Britains row includes such famous figures as, left to right, the 'plug-shouldered' lancer, the 'plug-handed' fusilier (to the right of its German look-alike), the 'Germanic' Life Guard, the 'plug-shouldered' Scots Grey and the 'plug-handed' highlanders, private and officer.*

BELOW: *Britains first set, Life Guards, the 'Germanic' model. The figures each had a tinplate sword, and the officer was one of the five with a gold sash. They are packed on paper and straw in exactly the same way as contemporary German figures.*

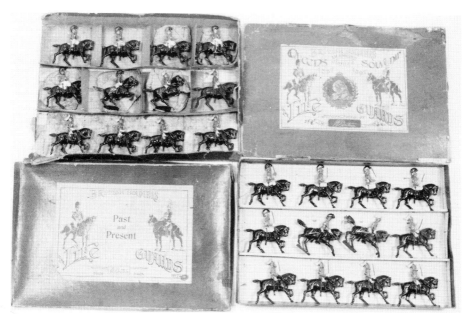

Early special occasion Britains. First made as a souvenir for Queen Victoria's Diamond Jubilee (top), the box shows the Life Guards in the uniforms of 1837 and 1897. The set was sufficiently popular to warrant continued production later as box number 72, Life Guards Past and Present (bottom). Note the thrifty re-use of most of the earlier label.

WILLIAM BRITAIN AND BRITAINS LTD

Because of extensive catalogue evidence and consistently numbered sets, Britains models are by far the best documented of all toy soldiers. The company still thrives and has been making toys since 1860, when William Britain senior (1826-1906), a toymaker all his life, founded the firm. In 1893 he and his family added toy soldiers to their range. Hollow casting was invented by them and this method of making hollow models enabled them to undercut the foreign competition by using less metal in the casting.

The name 'Britain' was a help to sales at a period when the British Empire was at its peak and emphasised that the models were British made. It can cause confusion, however, unless one is aware that the term Britains soldiers refers to the products of Britains Ltd, as distinct from British soldiers in general. The first models sold by Britains were Germanic in appearance, very similar to contemporary Heyde figures, but the business expanded rapidly, the models were redesigned, and by 1900 there were about one hundred sets available in the best quality series alone, all sold in distinctive red boxes. The Britains style had now evolved, and all figures were made to a height of 54 millimetres (2⅛ inches) for a foot soldier, which corresponds to model railway gauge 1. This scale has remained the most popular for toy and model soldiers in Britain and the United States ever since.

The enterprise was always a family business. In the next generation, William Britain junior is credited with inventing hollow casting and had a flair for producing the master figures. His name can be seen underneath many of the dated castings. His brother Alfred was the manufacturing organiser, and another brother,

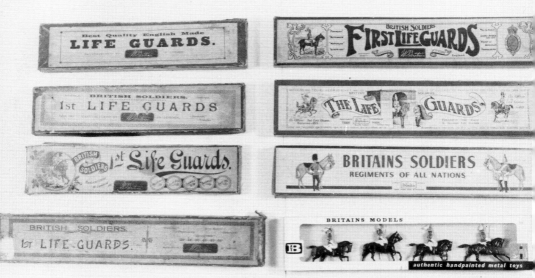

ABOVE: *A series of the different Britains boxes for set number 1, The Life Guards. On the left are three shorter boxes, all containing the 'Germanic' style figure, then a longer box with five of the larger 'tin sword' Life Guards. On the right at the top is the label designed by Fred Whisstock for the set. Next is the most attractive label that was current from about 1935 to 1952, after which the set went into a standard 'Regiments of All Nations' cavalry box. Finally, renumbered 9206, the set, now reduced to four pieces, appears in a 'window box'. None of the boxes on the left has the catalogue number 1 shown on it. Britains appear not to have numbered their range until about 1898.*

BELOW: *A series of Britains cavalry figures, featuring the Scots Greys. The sequence of figures in set 32 is shown after the 'plug-shouldered' first figure in the middle row. The top row shows B series figures, and the bottom row X, A and W series, all in second grade paint. In the middle row, the first 'tin sword' Scots Grey has a Foot Guards bearskin, but this is corrected in the second one. Then come a long rein and short rein version of the standard Scots Grey figure, followed by the new figures for trooper and officer added to the set about 1954, when Britains decided to give more variety to the five figures in each of their cavalry boxes.*

A series of Britains infantry, showing all the types of Fusiliers made, but including two Sussex Regiment (in the white helmets) to show the two marching infantry figures that did not appear with a Fusilier head. In the top row, all the Fusiliers except the last six are wearing gaiters. The first two figures on the left are with the 'Valise' pack.

Frederick, was the salesman. Two more brothers and two sisters all participated in the business in the early days of toy soldiers, but when success came they went their separate ways.

Britains' first set was a box of Life Guards, and their early soldiers were all depictions of the British Army in full dress. Once they had a reasonable range of these, often using contemporary prints by R. Simkin, issued with the *Army and Navy Gazette*, for inspiration and paint detail, they began to branch out following contemporary events: the South Australian Lancers at Queen Victoria's Jubilee, the 21st Lancers 'Heroes of Omdurman', the Boer War, the Cuban War, and so on. In 1940 the formation of the Home Guard was followed in three months by the issue of set 1918, the Home Guard in miniature. This was the last set issued before the firm went over to real war production, making parts for fuses, mines and bombs.

In 1900 Britains ordinary sets comprised eight figures (if foot soldiers with movable arms) or ten figures (if foot soldiers with fixed arms) or five cavalry figures, for a shilling a box. Boxes of second-grade fixed arm figures or the small-size figures (40 millimetres or 1½ inches scale) contained seven foot or four

cavalry to the box and cost 6d. These prices were held until the First World War. A set that had cost a shilling cost 1s 7½d in 1937, 5s 6d in 1950 and 12s 6d at the close of production in 1966.

The story of Britains can be divided into three eras, separated by the two world wars, each era then being subdivided into two periods. The transition between the six periods was gradual, however, for Britains were a commercial firm and were producing models in the most economical way rather than to help historians! Models originating in one period were therefore often produced well into a subsequent period until the moulds wore out, and this can cause confusion when trying to date a particular figure.

BEFORE THE FIRST WORLD WAR
First period. Early expansion, 1893-1900. Figures were mainly fixed-arm, oval-based, and with no marks under the base or horse's belly. There was frequent improvement of the figures. A few box labels were illustrated but most were made up of printer's type, hearts and flowers.
Second period. Dated production, 1900-16. Figures had copyright dates on paper

13

ABOVE: *Underneath the bases. Clues to identify and date Britains and other figures are often found underneath the bases. This row shows a paper label on a marching Cameron Highlander and the various engravings under charging Argyll and Sutherland Highlanders. The second and third figures are dated '17.12.1903', and when the oval base changed to a square shape the wording remained in oval form. The third figure has 'Made in Great Britain' added to the wording and the fifth figure has 'Made in England' upside down. The addition of these words was usually for export purposes.*

BELOW: *Different styles of highlanders by Britains. (Top left) An early box of Cameron Highlanders with smooth foreign service helmets. (Bottom left) Number 23B, small-size Camerons at the trail; the officer is the same figure with the rifle clipped off. Inexplicably this set is painted with Black Watch tartan kilts, whenever it appears. (Bottom right) A later version of the same set, now with correct Cameron kilts and a label designed by Fred Whisstock. (Top right) The same highlander figures in a second grade paint in box number 153W.*

A Britains cardboard fort from the 1940 catalogue. As these forts are rather fragile, not many have survived. The Royal West Surrey Regiment standing firing, which should be in the second row of the box, is missing. The fort folds up into the envelope bottom left and was then placed in the top of what was otherwise a normal Britains two-row box. The fort in the envelope was also available separately. Note that it was called a 'fort' on the box and a 'fortress' on the envelope.

labels or etched into the moulds. The date is always that when the master figure was made, not the date of production. The law was changed in 1911 so that this date on the figure was no longer necessary. From about 1913 box labels designed by Fred Whisstock, a freelance artist, later employed full time by Britains, were introduced.

BETWEEN THE WARS
First period. Consolidation, 1918-32. There was a gradual increase of the range, but much attention was given to building up the Home Farm series (not dealt with in this book). Whisstock continued to design box labels for new models.
Second period. Proliferation, 1932-41. There was a great increase of the range, particularly for export, stimulated by the coronation of King George VI and rearmament, with modern army troops, vehicles and guns. Whisstock labels were gradually replaced by new standard labels and a few illustrated designs.

In 1940 the catalogue contained these sections, which are listed with the number of lines produced in each section.
Modern army: artillery 27, Royal Air Force 7, anti-aircraft defence services 21, bands 5, cavalry 3, infantry 26, army transport and Royal Engineers 10, Royal Army Medical Corps 7, Royal Corps of Signals 1, tanks 3, large boxes 12, Royal Navy 13.
Ceremonial dress: artillery 6, bands 11, cavalry 25, infantry 39, army transport and Royal Engineers 3, Royal Army Medical Corps 3, Royal Navy 2, large boxes 45.
The British Empire: Africa 6, Australia 3, Canada 12, India 16, New Zealand 2, West Indies 1.
Armies of the world: Abyssinia 3, Argentina 3, Austria 4, Belgium 8, Bulgaria 1, China 1, Egypt 4, France 13, Germany 4, Greece 3, Irish Republic 1, Italy 8, Japan 3, Mexico 1, Poland 1, Spain 2, Turkey 2, Uruguay 3, United States of America 42, native warriors 12, types of the Wild West 25, Boy Scouts 4.
Historical series 17, *W series (small size)* 32, *A series (second grade)* 113, *army buildings* 26.
Total 644 items.
In addition, this catalogue contained seventy-six pages of farm, zoo and miscellaneous non-military items.

ABOVE: Paint styles in Britains Black Watch. The private on the left shows the standard of painting for normal production in the 1930s. He is probably from set number 449. Compare this with the better painted detail of the next three in line and the left-hand mounted officer, all of which are 'special paintings' done by Britains to customer's order. The drummer and piper on the right from set number 2109 and the mounted officer on the right from set number 2126 show the typical good Britains painting standard in the late 1950s. In contrast to the 1930s figures, there are no moustaches and the reins are not painted in on the horses.

RIGHT: *Britains set number 73. A spectacular full display box of Britains figures, dating from about 1901. Contents, from top to bottom: Band of the Line; 2nd Life Guards; Royal Welch Fusiliers; 17th Lancers; Gordon Highlanders; Royal Scots Greys; and Royal Horse Artillery, with a general. When the box was originally found some of the contents were missing, so others, matching as well as possible, had to be added to make up the correct number, e.g. the Gordon piper fourth from the right, which has much darker paint. The box is sturdily constructed of wood, with a sliding top (this was more often hinged). Later versions had cardboard lids, and from 1954 the whole box was made of cardboard.*

AFTER THE SECOND WORLD WAR

First period. Recovery, 1946-55. There was a shortage of sets available, but new sets began appearing in the 2000 range of numbers. There were no moustaches on figures from 1940 onwards. The new standardised 'Regiments of All Nations' range of full-colour box labels, was gradually introduced.

Second period. Competition with plastic figures and decline, 1955-66. Many more new sets were issued and new features included plastic drums on bandsmen, individual 'Picture Packs', half-size sets of four figures instead of eight, and 'window box' packing in 1960. The entire catalogue was renumbered in 1962 and sets became available only for export. The production of hollow-cast toy soldiers ended in 1966.

After the Second World War, an export-led revival in production took place, and the range continued to increase until 1958. New technology permitted the manufacture of models in plastic, and Britains were among the pioneers in plastic production through their acquisition of Herald in 1954. Over the next ten years the plastic models took over from the metal, as the plastic had the advantages of cheaper production, self-coloured material, lighter weight and greater durability, and a better quality of moulding undercuts could be used.

After 1966 the state coaches were the only metal models produced and they too were discontinued after two years. The last unpainted castings were sold, and the Britains original metal hollowcast became a limited edition after a total production of over a thousand million figures.

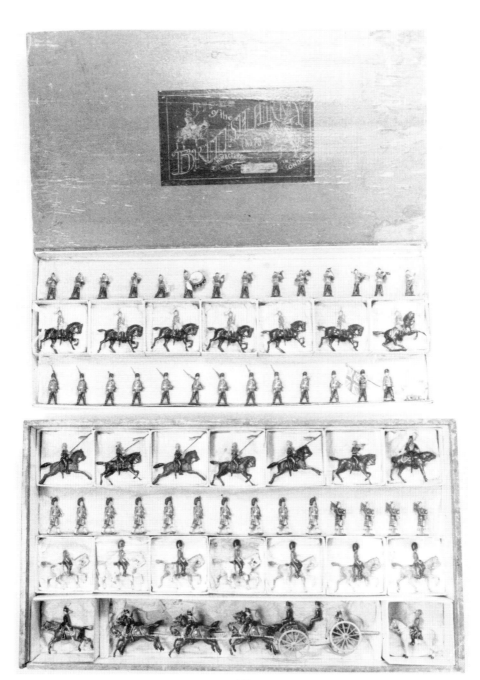

ABOVE: *Piracy. Of the two gun teams in this photograph the one in front is by Britains, but the rather battered one at the back is by Renvoize. The Renvoize drivers have movable arms, but otherwise the team and limber are almost identical to the Britains set. In the foreground is the Britains Royal Horse Artillery officer from the same set, followed by a Scots Grey obviously based on the same figure, but certainly not manufactured by Britains. A Hanks Brothers copy of Britains cavalry may be seen in the illustration on page 10 (top), top row at the right, copying a Britains South Australian Lancer.*

BELOW: *Box for Renvoize Russians, containing figures like the fourth from the left. Of the remaining figures, the two cavalry are attributed to Renvoize, figures two, five, seven and eight are by Hanks Brothers, and figures three, six and nine by Faudel Phillips. All are just sufficiently different from Britains to avoid prosecution for piracy.*

Cheap market-stall soldiers, two a penny, painted gold.

OTHER BRITISH MAKERS

William Britain's success with toy soldiers encouraged numerous imitators. Even German and French firms tried to copy the hollow-cast method, with various degrees of success. Many former employees of Britains started small businesses in East London, mostly supplying the cheaper products. Because these were often one-man businesses, records of their activities are hard to find, and they do not appear to have issued catalogues. Even to discover the names of the companies the best evidence comes from engraved trade marks on the figures, names on original boxes, and from citations in actions which Britains took against them when any of Britains' figures were copied too closely.

Britains were quick to counter this competition, both by introducing cheap sets of their own, and by rigorously prosecuting these 'pirates' wherever they were seen. Hanks Brothers and Company, in 1901, and James Renvoize, in 1902, were both taken to court for copying a Britains 'Imperial Yeoman'. Certainly, some of the copies produced were unjustly close to William Britain junior's originals. The problem of piracy was checked but reoccurs many times throughout the world. Following this defensive action by Britains, many of the competitors sought to establish distinctive styles of their own.

Of the early manufacturers, Hanks Brothers must have been among the first to judge from the number and variety of their models pirated from Britains. They used a different alloy to Britains, a metal which was shinier and caused the paint to flake off easily. James Renvoize, on the other hand, made superior models, and his citation as a pirate was an exception.

Reka Ltd, whose models are often marked 'C. W. Baker', seems to have produced a very large range, varying in quality from good to cheap. From the number of these models that still exist today, it seems that Reka was the most prolific competitor to Britains between 1905 and 1930. A number of the Reka moulds were redistributed to other companies in the early 1930s, possibly as a result of a bankruptcy sale. The precarious existence of these small companies is marked by a continuous redistribution of personnel and moulds. So great a number of different models, for instance of Household Cavalry, were issued under the Reka name, that their production

BMC sets in their boxes.

could hardly have been economic.

The firm known as BMC has recently been discovered to be the Brighton Model Company, although their address was in the East End of London, like so many other hollowcast manufacturers. They also produced lead warships and other toys. The figures produced were highly original, including a very fine series of armies of the world. Its figures tended to be rather larger than Britains'.

John Wood was a former employee of Britains who set up on his own. There appears to be just one figure of a Life Guard bearing the name 'J. Wood' before he and his brothers decided to name the company John Hill and Company with the trademark 'Johillco'. Their output before the First World War appears to have been small, but it increased between the wars. The company was sold in the late 1930s and started up again in 1947 in Burnley under new ownership, lasting until 1957.

The market for toy soldiers was very large during the first decade of the twentieth century. Encouragement seems to have come from the arms race with Germany, the successful conclusion of the Boer War, the spread of the Boy Scout movement, which had its own publication *War Games for Boy Scouts, Played with Model Soldiers*, which may well predate the more famous *Little Wars* by H. G. Wells published in 1913, and the promotional efforts of Britains themselves, who published their own wargaming booklet in 1908.

After the First World War a reaction set in against war toys and, although many were still sold, the main efforts of Britains and their rivals was in the development of more peaceful ranges outside the scope of this book. With the onset of rearmament, however, toy soldiers again came to the fore, and Johillco and the newcomer Crescent were most active, as were Taylor and Barratt, Kuzu and other companies, some of which produced soldiers as a sideline to ranges of model vehicles or other toys.

After the Second World War, there was a resurgence of interest in toy soldiers and, when supplies of lead alloy were once more available a number of new companies, notably Timpo, Charbens and Cherilea, joined in the market. As a result, the toy trade

20

ABOVE: *A 1918 cardboard toy. The soldiers stand up on wire clips; the scenery and ambulance are collapsible.*

BELOW: *Fry figures with their boxes. A speciality was made of First World War types. Some are simply painted gold.*

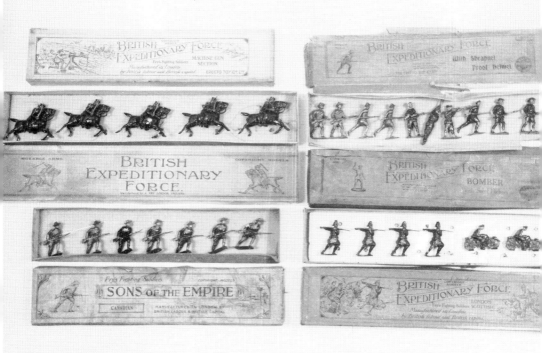

was split between the quality product, virtually the monopoly of Britains, though with brief incursions by Wend-Al (aluminium figures) and Timpo, and the cheaper soldiers sold through wholesalers, corner shops and Woolworths, where Hill (now under new management), Crescent, Charbens and Cherilea competed. Only the quality end, however, survived the introduction of plastic from 1954 onwards, and by 1959 Britains was the only firm still producing hollowcasts. All the others had, with more or less success, gone over to the new techniques.

A number of companies grew up in the north-west around Johillco, which had moved to Burnley. Their sales manager, Jim Leva, joined forces with Wilfred Cherrington, a freelance figure designer, to found the firm of Cherilea, and they eventually took over another short-lived company, the Fylde Manufacturing Company, also started by former Hill employees.

After the war both Britains and Hill began to use female outworkers, housewives who hand-painted models at home. In the north they were paid 6d per colour per hundred figures completed. Previously, all the large companies had employed women sitting in rows painting in the factory.

ABOVE: *Patriotic soldiers. The group on the left are Johillco, featuring a British lion. As with many cheap or souvenir lines, these are finished in gold paint. The soldiers on the right do not belong to the packing card, but they seem appropriate. The card dates from late 1939.*

BELOW: *Wend-Al figures of the early 1950s. Note Queen Elizabeth II on horseback and Winston Churchill. London's Household Division has always been a favourite for manufacturers to produce.*

ABOVE: *Early artillery to support the troops. A 54 millimetre scale Britains artillery officer shows the size of the guns. At the back are two gigantic guns suitable for knocking over toy soldiers at a distance, on the left made for Hamleys and on the right by OH and Company in their 'Unity' series. The other two guns on the left are made by Rivolet (SR), a French firm which made the French 75 millimetre field gun in many different sizes. The powerful looking gun in front on the right is the Britains Number 2 18-inch Howitzer on Field Carriage with its ammunition and loading plate. It cost 7s 6d, very expensive for those days. Finally, the Reka RHA gun in the centre had a label attached which reads: 'Projectiles shot from this gun will knock soldiers over instead of firing over their heads as the tall out of proportion guns do.'*

BELOW: *Timpo highlanders. Some on the left have flock-sprayed bonnets to give them a furry appearance. Although most represent Gordons, some of the tartans are odd. For instance, the two pipers on the left have purple and pink kilts.*

A selection of plastic types. To the left, a typical bag of soldiers from Hong Kong, as sold through the wholesale trade to local newsagents since the 1960s. These ones are pirated copies of Airfix. (Top row) Eaglewall figures from the 'Eagle' comic, of Dan Dare, his comrades and attendant space commandos, all made by Kentoy. The figure on the right is made in Turkey. (Middle row) The first figure is one of the first British-made plastics, a Malleable Mouldings guard, made in 1947. Next come four Kentoy guardsmen that are distinctly copies of Herald, and an Elastolin Norman and Saxon at the battle of Hastings. (Bottom row) A Roman, given free with a packet of cereal; a Mattel 'Hero' with movable waist and 'clicking sound' sub-machine gun; to the front a Kentoy military policeman, with three Aztecs, also by Kentoy; at the back a Marx caricature of a Japanese officer; at the right a group of infantry from Brazil copied from American metal 'dime store' figures and at the end a French St Cyr cadet, bought, and possibly made, in Russia.

PLASTIC TOY SOLDIERS

While Britains bought the firm of Herald making plastic models, and continued to produce metal soldiers as well, most other companies had a very short period of transition to plastic since the plastic product had a number of commercial advantages. Being flexible, plastic appeared to be much less breakable if handled roughly, and the purchaser had no cause to fear lead poisoning. Plastic models were thought of as 'safe' and 'unbreakable', although neither word was strictly accurate, and they soon dominated the market.

Toy soldier firms that successfully made the transition included Timpo, Cherilea and Crescent. Hill made the attempt, but after a year or so gave up. Some firms simply converted production of their existing models to plastic: others used completely new master figures for the new material. A number of new firms

also started, notably Lone Star. Plastic was not a British invention, as hollowcast was, and companies all over the world were using plastic before the British. The result has been that there are even more plastic models than there are metal. As with so many other products, cheap supplies from the newly industrialised countries, particularly Hong Kong, began to undercut the British-produced lines.

A further development was that, in contrast to metal, plastic toy soldiers could be sold unpainted and could thus be said to be a creative toy, in that the purchaser was asked to do the painting. The unpainted figures cost less and even began to be used as free gifts in cereal packets. In the United States the unpainted figure was the usual product of Marx, the leading manufacturer, sold in bags of a hundred men for one dollar. In Britain the unpainted figure was pioneered in the mid 1960s by Airfix, previously a maker of plastic model kits. The earliest sets from Airfix were in 20 millimetre (¾ inch, 00 gauge) scale, but later 54 millimetre sets and vehicles were also produced. Over a period of twenty-five years, from 1956 to 1981, cheap imported toys and unpainted models gradually forced the original painted models off the market. Even Britains, among others, had plastic soldiers made for them in Hong Kong.

Another possibility of plastic was the idea of more movable parts. Britains soldiers had always been famous for their movable arms, but Britains new plastic Swoppets, introduced as part of the expansion of the Herald line, had movable waists and necks, with many removable parts. Plastic soldiers with movable parts soon became widespread (and losing parts became a problem). Swoppets also had the advantage that each different part could be made in a different colour plastic, and so part of the painting could be eliminated. Timpo also experimented with a process of pouring more than one colour of plastic into the same mould, to create 'pre-coloured' figures.

The most impressive of all plastic toy soldiers were the Britains 'Eyes Right' range, Swoppet related figures with movable neck and arms. The bandsmen in this range had metal instruments, which fitted into the plastic arms at the wrist, and were metal-plated. These are acknowledged by toy soldier collectors and military modellers to be the finest band figures ever produced.

Since the demise of Timpo in 1979, Airfix figures and a reduced remnant of the Britains 'Deetail' range have been almost the only toy soldiers on the market, apart from cheap imports and a certain distribution by Matchbox (Lesney) and Atlantic (from Italy), both also with unpainted troops. The interest in collecting toy soldiers, however, appears to have increased as the toy market itself has declined, possibly because many of today's collectors were young in the boom period of 1950-65, and many of these new collectors are interested in collecting plastic figures.

RARITIES

With the phasing out of the much loved lead soldiers, a number of people started to collect them in earnest. The lead soldier, no longer in commercial production, began to acquire a rarity value, and the collector's market has been expanding since around 1970, with its own specialist dealers and auctions.

Toy soldiers that are *rare* are those that are very seldom seen at auctions or mentioned in dealers' lists. They may have been manufactured only for a short time, been an unpopular toy, or been so cheap as to have been regarded as expendable. Some sets of Britains soldiers are rare in Britain because they were all exported. To the knowledgeable collector of rarities, some sets are rare but relatively cheap, as most collectors do not realise they exist. Prices depend on a combination of the rarity and the demand from collectors. For example, Britains set number 2111, Colour Party of the Black Watch, with six figures in it, has fetched £290 at auction, yet is available ten times more often than set number 2119, the Scots Greys at attention, which in the same sale fetched only £40. This simply means that many more collectors would like to own the colour party than desire the Scots Greys.

Since nine-tenths of the British market in old toy soldiers is made up of Britains figures, these will be examined in some detail with regard to what is rare and valuable. First, however, here are a few general principles that apply to all toy soldiers. Although it is acceptable to collect toy soldiers in any condition, collectors prefer complete sets in good condition, without breakages, repairs or retouching of the paintwork, and in their original boxes. The best and most valuable sets are those boxed and looking just as they did when they were on display in the toyshop.

A rare 'Germanic' set of Britains 12th Lancers, 'plug-shouldered'.

Although repainted and repaired toy soldiers are not as valuable as originals, any odd figure broken or in poor paint condition (50 per cent of paint missing) will not usually lose value by being repaired or retouched. However, it would be unwise to try to repair faults in an otherwise good original set, as collectors prefer a defect to a repair. Equally, unusual figures, or any that cannot immediately be identified, could be rarities, and rarities should not be repaired or repainted since they indicate what a good figure should look like, as long as they remain untouched.

For Britains soldiers, in general terms, the older the set, the rarer it will be. The oldest boxes are those which have no set number on them. Britains first numbered their sets about 1898, when the first eighty or so sets were already on the market. All the sets produced before the First World War (sets 1 to 191) are considered to be rare, particularly if in their original boxes, but these same set numbers were often produced right up to 1961. The rarities are the actual figures

produced before 1916. Extremely rare are the figures produced in this period by a branch that Britains set up in Paris, which made several models never sold in Britain. Sets produced before 1905 are also extremely rare and always command a good price. Early Britains figures often do not possess the distinctive movable arm of the later standard figures, but many of the early moulds were used later to produce second-grade figures, and many of the figures in action poses never had movable arms. First-grade Britains were very well painted compared to most of the competition and second grades. Faces included eyes, eyebrows, moustaches, pink cheeks and hair at the nape of the neck. Uniforms included jacket buttons and stripes down the side of the trousers. Paintings more recent than the First World War tend to be brighter and harsher in appearance, and most of the eyebrows and, from 1940, the moustaches are gone.

The following types of Britains sets are likely to be both rare and desirable: soldiers depicting the Boer War; early

British and Empire troops; armies of the world, particularly Spain, Prussia, Austria and the Balkan states; novelty items such as sets 25, 72, 148 and 149; unnumbered items specially cast or painted by Britains to special order. Unfortunately no records of these have yet been unearthed, and they can only be recognised by their non-standard casting, uniform or paint quality.

Other areas particularly popular with collectors are highlanders, British cavalry, troops of the British Indian Empire, and horse-drawn guns and vehicles.

A number of firms are making toy-style figures in metal, not as children's toys, but to add to the collections of toy soldier enthusiasts. Although these do not come strictly within the definition of 'toy soldiers', they can often fill gaps in a collection where genuine toy manufacturers never made certain items. An example might be artillery for the Boers, in a display of toy soldiers depicting the Boer War. The collector who is prepared to paint the figures himself can buy them more cheaply unpainted. Model shops often stock some of these figures, and advertisements for them appear in specialist magazines.

ABOVE: *A Britains souvenir model of HIH Wilhelm II, 'Kaiser Bill', before the First World War. Note that the Britains name and trademark do not appear. The figure is a standard dragoon officer of the period, in a copper finish, which looks dull silver, with gilt detail.*

BELOW: *The famous Jameson Raid took place in 1895-6, and Britains produced this souvenir box. Later, Dr Jameson was dropped from the box title which became set number 38, South African Mounted Infantry.*

ABOVE: *Types of the Boer War. The Boer infantry is on the left, at the top showing the various arms fitted to the marching figure (a rifle at the trail arm was also used), and at the bottom showing the on guard, at the shoulder and officer figures. The British in foreign service helmets are in the top row: (left to right) 6th Dragoon, York and Lancaster Regiment, Gloucestershire Regiment in early and late version, Dublin Fusilier, Devonshire Regiment, Dublin with later version helmet, Devons with later helmet at the slope and the trail, and Cameron Highlander. In the bottom row are the British in slouch hats: (left to right) City Imperial Volunteer, Imperial Yeoman, officer and men at the trail to go with the Army Service Supply Column wagon at the back. The box lid for this is shown above. The full set was two wagons, ten men marching and the officer. It was not sold as a Britains set but supplied under the CFE label.*

BELOW: *Early box lids for some of the Boer War sets.*

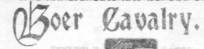

ABOVE: *Britains set number 25, Soldiers to Shoot. In standard 54 millimetre scale, the gun is hollow, and a thin wire 'bullet' is inserted at the shoulder. The steel spring is then flicked to propel the 'bullet' from the front of the gun barrel. Produced 1895-1916.*

ABOVE: *Britains Royal Lancaster Regiment. Britains set number 148, a patented game in which the bases are inserted in hinged clips that tip back when the soldier is knocked over by gunfire. When the board is tipped, the soldiers all stand up again automatically. There is a theory that Britains decided to change all their bases from oval to square to be able to fit them in these clips.*

ABOVE: *A Britains special box, the Royal Marine Colour Party, produced in small numbers for sale exclusively through Hamleys in 1939. Note the unnumbered box, which would normally have a number stamped in the seal illustrated hanging from the scroll on the lid.*

*(Top row) A group of Chinese soldiers of the Boxer Rebellion period, commissioned by the author.
(Bottom row) Types of the forces participating in the Peking Relief Expedition during the Boxer
Rebellion: United States, Austria, Russia, Japan, Prussia, France and Italy. These are by Bastion
figures.*

IDENTIFICATION, PURCHASE AND CARE

Here are a few hints on how to tell the type, manufacturer and age of any toy soldier, with suggestions on acquisition, storage, repair and improvement.

Type. The type of toy soldier should fall into one of the seven categories described in the second chapter, where the characteristics of each method of manufacture are given.

Manufacturer. Look first underneath the base of the figure or, if there is no base, under the belly of the horse. If there is no name or mark, there may be one elsewhere, along the inside leg or down the side of a saddlecloth, for instance. Looking at the base should reveal clearly the type of metal used and the casting method. This and the style of model, painting and even the form of such words as 'Made in England' may enable it to be matched with some other model the manufacturer of which is known. Even so many items do still remain unidentified.

Age. It is usually evident from the consistency of the paint used which of the three twentieth-century eras a figure is from. In the absence of the better clues furnished by Britains figures, the more detailed the painting, the earlier it usually is. Some paints look 'plastic', and figures painted in these are either repainted or post Second World War. A figure in pristine condition is unlikely to date from before the First World War. Plastic figures are all more recent than the Second World War. Any box label in full colour is not likely to be earlier than 1950.

Acquisition. There are various methods of buying toy soldiers:
1. From relatives or friends.
2. By advertising from members of the public (prices subject to negotiation).
3. By swopping, buying and selling with other collectors. It is best to join a local branch of the British Model Soldier Society. Write to the Secretary, David Pearce, 22 Lynwood Road, Ealing, London W5 1JJ, for details.
4. By attending auctions. The best ones are held by Phillips Auctioneers in central London every two months. Prices can be high for the better items, but interest-

ing large mixed lots can prove a bargain. The view days are also good opportunities to look at some thousands of models at a time and are open for anyone to come and see.

5. From specialist dealers. Expensive though usually reliable, whether purchases are made by post or from antique stalls, for instance in Greys Antique Market or the Portobello Road in London. Details of dealers can be found in *Bulletin* (the magazine of the British Model Soldier Society), *Toy Soldier Parade* magazine, or by subscribing to an American publication, the *Old Toy Soldier Newsletter*, 209 North Lombard, Oak Park, Illinois 60302, USA.

6. By visiting antique shops and charity shops, attending swapmeets, looking in *Exchange and Mart* and local newspapers, and so on. These methods are probably cheap, but are time-consuming.

Storage. Toy soldiers must all be treated with care. Because chalk was often mixed with the plastic, to help the adhesion of the paint, plastic models can be more fragile than metal figures. An even room temperature, good ventilation of cabinets, avoidance of oak furniture, and the use of cardboard boxes and tissue paper (never any kind of plastic bags or wrapping) will all help to preserve metal soldiers, either on display or in boxes. Damp and sunlight are the great enemies, causing 'lead disease' and paint fading respectively. Kept in good conditions, figures with these defects should not deteriorate further.

Repairs. The best way of doing repairs is by cannibalising the most damaged figures to mend the better ones. Sometimes, recast spare parts can be obtained, and it can be well worth while to learn hand casting or to encourage a dextrous friend to take it up. Loose hollow-cast heads are traditionally replaced using a matchstick cut to fit in the hollow neck. Composition figures can be repaired with plastic wood. Metal figures with dents or holes benefit from repairs with a metal filler such as Milliput. Soldering parts together is the way to make most permanent metal repairs, but low temperature solder must be used. Ordinary impact adhesive is effective if haste is necessary and epoxy resin can be satisfactory, although cyanoacrylates react with lead and do not form a permanent bond.

Conversions. An excellent way of building up an attractive group of figures is to convert models, broken or otherwise, to poses never originally made by the manufacturer. Britains cavalry, for instance, can by this method be given officers, trumpeters and standard bearers which were never included in the original sets. This sort of work, however, and the creation of scenic settings for the attractive display of models, is a modelmaker's craft and outside the scope of this book.

An example of a small speciality collection of figures, officers with binoculars, which include representatives from many different manufacturers.

PLACES TO VISIT

GREAT BRITAIN

Bethnal Green Museum of Childhood, Cambridge Heath Road, London E2 9PA. Telephone: 081-980 4315. Earlier Britains figures and part of BMSS National Collection.

London Toy and Model Museum, 23 Craven Hill, London W2 3EN. Telephone: 071-262 7905 or 9450.

National Army Museum, Royal Hospital Road, London SW3 4HT. Telephone: 071-730 0717.

National Collection of the British Model Soldier Society, Hatfield House, Hatfield, Hertfordshire. Telephone: 0707 262823. Most of the National Collection of the BMSS.

Newhaven Fort, Fort Road, Newhaven, East Sussex BN9 9DL. Telephone: 0273 517622.

Tower 73, The Wish Tower, King Edward's Parade, Eastbourne, East Sussex. Telephone: 0323 410300. Part of the BMSS National Collection is displayed here.

York Castle Museum, Tower Street, York YO1 1RY. Telephone: 0904 653611.

OTHER COUNTRIES

Forbes Collection, Palais Mendoub, Tangier, Morocco. One of the world's largest public displays of toy soldiers, with well over seventy thousand figures.

Forbes Magazine Collection, 60 Fifth Avenue, New York, USA. Over ten thousand figures are displayed.

A number of military and municipal museums also have collections of toy soldiers.

FURTHER READING

Asquith, Stuart. *The Collector's Guide to New Toy Soldiers*. Argus, 1991.

Fontana, Dennis. *The War Toys No 2: The Story of Lineol*. New Cavendish, 1991.

Garratt, John G. *The World Encyclopaedia of Model Soldiers*. Muller, 1981.

Goldberg, Muriel. *The Toy Collectors' Handbook*. Goldfinch, 1992.

Joplin, Norman. *British Toy Figures, 1900 to the present*. Arms and Armour Press. 1987.

Joplin, Norman. *A History of British Hollowcast Figures*. New Cavendish, 1992.

O'Brien, Richard. *Collecting Toy Soldiers*. Books Americana, 1988.

Opie, James. *Britains Toy Soldiers, 1893-1932*. Gollancz, 1985.

Opie, James. *British Toy Soldiers, 1893 to the Present*. Arms and Armour Press, 1985.

Opie, James. *Collecting Toy Soldiers*. Collins, 1987.

Opie, James. *The Great Book of Britains, 100 Years of Toy Soldiers, 1893-1992*. New Cavendish, 1993.

Ortmann, Erwin. *Model Tin Figures*. Studio Vista, 1974.

Polaine, Reggie. *The War Toys No 1: The Story of Hausser-Elastolin*. New Cavendish, 1979.

Rose, Andrew. *The Collector's All-Colour Guide to Toy Soldiers*. Salamander, 1985.

Wallis, Joe. *Regiments of All Nations*. Private publication, 1980. Britains figures, military and civilian, produced after the Second World War.

Private publications, reprinted catalogues, periodicals and other useful literature can often be obtained from dealers or at meetings of the British Model Soldier Society, Honorary Curator, John Ruddle, telephone: 081 979 7137. Back numbers of the catalogues of toy soldier auctions, together with the prices realised, may be purchased from Phillips Auctioneers. That of the Richards Collection is the most useful and contains ninety-nine photographs.

Information about *Plastic Warrior*, a newsletter for plastic toy soldier collectors, can be obtained from Paul Morehead, 65 Watton Court, Woking, Surrey.